HOPES AND DREAMS THAT SOUND LIKE YOURS

Stories of Queer Activism in Sub-Saharan Africa

Published by

Taboom Media & GALA Queer Archive

2021

First Published in 2021 by MaThoko's Books
PO Box 31719, Braamfontein, 2017, South Africa

MaThoko's Books is an imprint of GALA Queer Archive

ISBN: 978-0-620-93534-0 (print)

Editing, stories, artwork, cover design, and book design by Taboom Media and GALA Queer Archive

CONTRIBUTORS

Editor: Brian Pellot

Assistant Editor: Debra L. Mason

Contributing Editors: Isabella Matambanadzo, Wana Udobang

Authors: Dzoe Ahmad, S.E.B., David Ochara, Bulelani Mzila, Pamina Sebastião, Bakang Ndaba, Timiebi Ebitibituwa, David Larbi, "Mystique", Jenneh Mustapha, Mike Daemon, Kashindi Shabani Gady, Frank Lileza, Sulemani Muhirwa, Stephen Okwany, Uchenna Samuel Ngene, Eppy Mutetwa, DK Dlamini, Gigie, Nandini Tanya Lallmon, Charles Mukoma, Brian Pellot, Karin Tan

Illustrators: Khanya Kemani, Lamb of Lemila, Amina Gimba, Lame Dilotsotlhe, Mercy Thokozane Minah, Neil Badenhorst, Annabela Bekker, Larissa Mwanyama, Naadira Patel

Design and Cover Illustration: Naadira Patel

Project Managers: Brian Pellot and Karin Tan

To view or download a digital version of this guide, please visit:
TaboomMedia.com
GALA.co.za

First published in 2021
Taboom Media
GALA Queer Archive
Cape Town, South Africa

Publication was made possible with funding from the Arcus Foundation and the National Endowment for Democracy. Additional support provided by the Rosa Luxemburg Stiftung (RLS) with funds from the Federal Ministry of Economic Cooperation and Development of the Federal Republic of Germany. The contents of this publication are the sole responsibility of its authors and do not necessarily represent the views of funding partners.

CONTENTS

A brief note on abbreviations:

The words and abbreviations used to describe sexual and gender diversity vary across context and culture. Some activists work on "LGBT rights," others for "LGBTQI+ equality." Throughout this anthology, each individual author's preferred terms and abbreviations have been preserved.

FOREWORD

"Our growing archive linked past stories to present selves. We became part of an African movement to tell and preserve queer stories, writing our existence into history."
— Pamina Sebastião, Arquivo de Identidade Angolano

The above quote from Pamina Sebastião's story, *Building a Body, Telling Our Story,* resonates closely with work the GALA Queer Archive has been doing since the late 1990s. It speaks to the radical act of individuals taking ownership of history-making.

Storytelling uses our present experiences and imagined futures to build a broader narrative of history. As queer people, as African people, our lives and stories are often erased or omitted from historical narratives in an attempt to invalidate our existence. GALA's archive, oral history projects, youth empowerment workshops, and other educational programming help queer people tell our stories and insert ourselves into broader conversations. Recording and sharing our lives by defiantly and confidently "writing our existence into history" counteracts the erasure we've long faced.

The stories in this anthology offer a range of "making-of" vignettes. They describe how individual queer activists in Sub-Saharan Africa have come to be where they are today. Some stories touch on personal themes of religion and faith, coming out, mental health, and friendship. Other stories reflect the broader context and struggles human rights organisations face when working in countries that perpetrate violence and enforce discriminatory laws against queer people. The authors of these stories — identifying as lesbian, bisexual, gay, transgender,

gender non-conforming, and ally — depict queer African experiences as nuanced and diverse, neither singular nor linear.

Bulelani Mzila's story recounts hearing rumours about famous South Africans being queer. Although these rumours were whispered in their community, the message Bulelani heard was loud and clear, "people like me existed." It is through the proliferation of stories like the ones found in this anthology — stories that are not rumours, that are not whispered — that we are able to build a complex and undeniable testament to our existence.

More often than not, "making-of" queer stories are characterised by experiences of hardship and pain, of rejection and discrimination. The stories in this anthology, though sometimes difficult to confront, all come with messages of hope. In the face of overwhelming adversity, it is natural for us to read the experiences of these activists as resilient and resistant. Despite their challenging circumstances, they're accelerating change through education, advocacy, archiving, storytelling, relief aid, health care, and legislative action. Every bit counts.

Hopes and Dreams That Sound Like Yours: Stories of Queer Activism in Sub-Saharan Africa highlights some of the necessary work happening on the continent to advance queer rights and combat discrimination. The anthology reveals how positive change comes from both collective action and a collection of actions. If we extend this message of collective history-making, we come to understand that within our queerness, we are connected.

Instead of allowing history to retroactively explain who we are, let us write and build our own nuanced history by telling our individual and collective stories.

Karin Tan
Senior Information Officer
GALA Queer Archive
May 2021, Johannesburg

INTRODUCTION

In January 2021, Taboom Media assembled more than 30 activists from 18 countries in Sub-Saharan Africa for a week-long media advocacy workshop. Our goal was to help regional human rights defenders create and implement their own media campaigns to advance LGBTQI+ equality.

The meeting was originally scheduled for Cape Town, but COVID-19 forced us to gather on Zoom instead. We logged on from laptops and smartphones, our floating pixelated heads tiled across the screen, scattered across the continent.

Part of what makes Taboom's workshops with journalists and activists so special is everything that happens outside the classroom. On Zoom we can walk you through the fundamentals of media advocacy, but we can't laugh together over coffee, strategise over dinner, or commiserate over shared struggles.

We started the week with low expectations. Zoom fatigue is real. Internet struggles are real. Would anyone show up? Would anyone care?

Yes and yes. More activists than we hoped. More deeply than we dreamed.

Hopes and Dreams That Sound Like Yours: Stories of Queer Activism in Sub-Saharan Africa emerged from this workshop for one reason — we weren't done sharing our stories. Each activist wanted to better understand what inspired the rest to join our collective fight for equality. On the final day, we asked everyone to write down their activist journeys or "stories of change." Those initial responses became early drafts that laid the groundwork for this anthology.

We spent the next two months interviewing each activist to expand and refine their stories. Through video calls, text messages, voice notes, and edits back and forth, we got to know each other more intimately than a week of Zoom webinars could ever allow.

A beautiful queer archive was taking shape, so we reached out to GALA to see how we might collaborate and share these stories. We landed on the idea of commissioning queer and ally artists to produce original illustrations for each story and then packaging everything together into an anthology of bravery and resilience.

More than 40 people contributed to *Hopes and Dreams* and its accompanying videos over three short months. We kept a tight schedule in order to launch ahead of the International Day Against Homophobia, Biphobia, Intersexism, and Transphobia (IDAHOBIT) on May 17. We hope that our collective efforts honour this year's theme: "Together: Resisting, Supporting, Healing!"

COVID-19 kept us socially distanced but never apart. Few of us have met in person, but our community thrives online. This anthology brought us together.

Like many of the stories it contains, *Hopes and Dreams* presents a silver lining, something beautiful and inspiring that emerged from a difficult year of loss and isolation. Its title comes from a line in David Ochara's story, *Just Knock and You Can Enter:*

"We're sharing our hopes and dreams — hopes and dreams that sound like yours."

Whoever you are, wherever you're from, whatever your background, we invite you to find yourself in these stories.

At their core, our hopes and dreams are universal.

Our hopes and dreams are yours.

Brian Pellot
Anthology Editor and Project Manager
Founding Director at Taboom Media
May 2021, Cape Town

ZIMBABWE
opener
TREAT
MENTAL HEALTH
Hope
Worthy
LGBTI
Love
worth
power

I'M A TRANS WOMAN. I'M WORTHY OF LOVE.

DZOE AHMAD
Zimbabwe

Our bodies are not designed by craftsmen. They reflect how we feel. They affirm our individuality.

I was born in Esigodini, a small mining town in Zimbabwe where drunkards murder each other to steal gold mine territory. It was hell on Earth. Poverty and hardship were all around me. Fear sat close to my heart.

This toxic environment seeped into my soul. I survived by denying my true identity as a transgender girl and tolerating the shameful names people called me: "stabane," "ncukubili," "wule." I created a hard shell to protect me from the outside world, but it also prevented me from embracing my truth.

My mother always said, "exposure is an eye-opener." Turns out she was right!

In 2018 I moved to Zimbabwe's second-largest city Bulawayo. At first I was afraid of the speeding cars and the street vendors' shouts. I was just a trans girl from a small town. Being in the city meant boldly navigating unfamiliar spaces and protecting myself from the gaze of strangers. But soon some of these strangers became friends.

Illustration by Amina Gimba

I was introduced to Trans Research Education Advocacy & Training (TREAT), a transgender rights group in Bulawayo that works to prevent human rights violations across Zimbabwe. There I met people like me, my trans sisters. They didn't apologise or make excuses for who they were. They were living their truths. I was shocked to see such freedom in

Zimbabwe. Was I in Johannesburg? Was I dreaming? How could people live so openly? For people with knowledge of the law, for people who understood human rights, my childhood dream was already a reality. I felt born again.

I broke into tears of joy, but truly my emotions were mixed. My president, my community, my country had always told me that LGBTI people are worse than pigs and dogs. But at TREAT, people like me told me I was beautiful and worthy. My mind was racing. I needed answers. Who was I?

In 2019 1 was appointed as TREAT's programmes coordinator and started working to empower human rights defenders to improve legislative frameworks and non-discriminatory environments for LGBTI persons in Southern Africa. As my work with TREAT advanced, so did my gender transition. I crafted a Hollywood image for myself. I aimed for perfection. I went above and beyond in everything I did, but I forgot to take care of my mental health.

Enter 2020.

The COVID pandemic sent Zimbabwe into lockdown. I couldn't access my expensive hormones from Botswana. The body 1 had spent years refining and perfecting to affirm my gender identity started disappearing into thin air. Months went by. 1 lost hope. My self-esteem plummeted. This new reality became a nightmare.

And then I started reflecting. I asked the walls of my apartment, "Why do we spend so much money on things that are temporary?" There was no response.

Trans people change their bodies to gain affirmation. From themselves? From society? But how do we transform our souls?

As I lost some of my gender-affirming body features, I gained an appreciation for how diverse and wide the trans spectrum truly is. If trans people I know and love can be happy in all different shapes and stages and sizes, why can't l?

Sitting alone at home, watching my body change against my will, I learned the power of self-worth and self-love. No matter how I look,

I am a trans woman, and I am worthy of love. That's my "pillow" of strength. I learned to find happiness in my current situation rather than dwelling on a dwindling past that would hurt my present.

I'm comfortable on the wide streets of Bulawayo now. Traffic lights click from yellow to red, but I stay focused on the green lights that keep me going. Hormones or not, I've found my true self.

Our bodies mean nothing without the right mindset. If we create positive narratives, if we nurture our mental health, we can find inner peace and radiate love to the world.

Let your inner beauty shine out.

Dzoe Ahmad is the former programmes coordinator at Trans Research Education Advocacy & Training (TREAT) in Bulawayo, Zimbabwe. She now serves as co-programmes manager at Gender DynamiX in Cape Town, South Africa.

I FLED SUDAN FOR A LIFE WORTH LIVING

S.E.B.
Uganda

I was born in a humble home in Khartoum to a Sudanese mother and a Ugandan father. The two branches of my family fought about most things, but they always agreed on me. As a young girl, they loved my bubbly personality. As a queer woman, they branded me the devil's daughter, hell-bent on "spoiling and recruiting innocent children."

I'm not the only outsider in my family. My mum's parents begrudgingly accepted my Ugandan dad because he's Muslim, but he never felt welcome in Sudan. Fed up after a decade of ethnic discrimination and judgement in Khartoum, he moved my family to the U.S. soon after I was born.

You might think someone who fled persecution would develop some tolerance for diversity. Not my dad. When I was six years old we were watching the evening news when colourful images of Washington, D.C.'s gay pride parade flashed across the screen. Dad immediately changed the channel and started screaming homophobic insults. "Daddy, why are you angry at people for jumping and dancing?" I asked. He muttered something about how America was ruining his children's minds. Soon we were on a plane to Eritrea, our lives reset once more.

As a teenager in Eritrea, I realised I was attracted to women. "It's just a phase, it will pass," I told myself. When it didn't, I did what African Muslim teens are trained to do: I prayed the bad spirits away and ignored

Illustration by Lamb of Lemila

my desires. I started dating men, trying to rewire my brain and my heart, but nothing worked.

Years passed, but that newscast I watched as a child never left me. My father's anger at seeing queer joy still vexed me. How could dad hate these strangers for accepting themselves, for finding happiness, for living authentically?

His anger hurt because I knew I was one of them. I too wanted to live openly, honestly, joyfully — as a lesbian woman — and I wanted others to find the same freedom. I moved back to Sudan to start a career in humanitarian development with a clear focus on combatting discrimination in all its forms.

As soon as I arrived back in Khartoum I came out to my friends as a proud lesbian. I thought they would accept me and that their acceptance would give me the courage to come out to my parents and stop all the pretending. I thought wrong.

My "friends" harassed me. Some tried to take me to healers to "cure my disease." Others refused to see me, worried "the bad omens God was bestowing on me" would find them too. In the end, only two friends stuck by my side. The others gossiped about my sexual orientation all over town, and word eventually reached my office. I was fired. I'd only joined to "recruit other girls and destroy their future," my boss said as I left the office for the last time.

Losing my job stung, but the year only got worse. I was arrested twice in 2013, the first time for "supporting homosexuality," the second time for having coffee with a human rights activist who works to reform anti-LGBTQI+ laws in Sudan. I spent more than three weeks in jail and am still traumatised by the torture and insults I received just for expressing my true self.

By that point, I thought my life was over. I kept working to support human rights but privately fell into a deep depression. Eventually the fog lifted enough for me to see things clearly and make some important decisions.

First, I decided to leave Islam. I could no longer be part of a religious community that did not accept my existence. Then I decided to leave

Sudan. The country of my birth had nearly destroyed me, and I needed a fresh start. I moved to Uganda in 2018 in search of freedom and have been advocating from here ever since.

Although Uganda's queer community faces enormous challenges, we find strength in unity. The hardships I faced in Sudan now give me strength to fight for our basic rights, dignity, and equality, and to move society towards not just tolerating us, but accepting our full humanity too.

My father fled Sudan for a better life he never found. I fled Sudan for a life worth living. I'm fighting for change so we don't have to flee again.

S.E.B. is communication manager at FEM Alliance Uganda, an organisation established in 2011 to represent the needs of Uganda's LBTQ community.

JUST KNOCK AND YOU CAN ENTER

DAVID OCHARA
Kenya

The year is 2013. A group of young Kenyans sits clustered in a basement apartment in Nairobi. We're playing games, catching up, hanging out. We're sharing our hopes and dreams — hopes and dreams that sound like yours.

We're just like you, we are you, but Kenyan society says we're "different." Our difference is what unites us. We're queer. Not "queer" in the strange way society thinks. "Queer" in the way we've reclaimed that word. We're lesbian, gay, bisexual, transgender, intersex. We're sexual and gender minorities who have found friendship, acceptance, and understanding in each other's company, in each other's shared experiences.

We start talking about religion. Someone mentions a recent survey that showed 97 percent of Kenyans identify as religious and more than 90 percent believe homosexuals should not be accepted in our society. That number hurts, but we're not surprised. Our group's collective experience with religion up to this point has been hatred, rejection, condemnation, and confusion.

Ciku's mom, a church treasurer, told her to ditch her queer friends. Oketch's pastor told him to come out of Sodom and seek God's salvation. Kwame tried to "fast the gay away" so many times his health started deteriorating from malnutrition.

Illustration by Neil Badenhorst

It's a sickening truth that we spent most of our early lives serving and strengthening religious institutions that treat queer people as outsiders or enemies, that subject us to spiritual violence.

Most of us quit the religious groups we grew up in. Most of us can't even remember the last time we stepped into a place of worship. The trauma is too raw, the rejection too painful. Yet we still feel connected to a greater power, still crave a community centred around something bigger than ourselves.

Our tense situation reminds me of the gospel song "Appointment" by Kenyan artist Jimmy Gait. The song is about two friends. One becomes a successful businessman while the other struggles to make ends meet. When the poor friend calls on his rich friend at work for help, the secretary and security guards won't let him in. Hopeless, he turns to God and finds peace. God doesn't require appointments; just knock and you can enter.

As friends and I listened to this song on repeat over the next few months, we realised we didn't need our existing churches or our pastors' approval to receive God's love. As a queer community, we could create and nourish our own authentic and healthy relationships with God. But it wouldn't be easy.

Next door in Uganda, national debate on an anti-homosexuality bill had reached fever pitch. Disinformation, religious bigotry, and political scapegoating led to early drafts of the bill that included the death penalty — quite literally a "Kill the Gays" bill. We feared for our neighbours' lives and worried this anti-LGBTIQ rhetoric might spill into Kenya.

Around that time we met Bishop Joseph W. Tolton from The Fellowship of Affirming Ministries (TFAM), a group of mostly African American Christian leaders who promote radical inclusivity. Bishop Tolton was working with grassroots activists across East Africa to protect queer Ugandans. He encouraged us to formalise our basement gatherings and make them more accessible, so in November 2013 we moved to a queer-affirming venue and held our first official worship service as the Cosmopolitan Affirming Community (CAC).

We created CAC to reclaim our spirituality and faith traditions. Our small group of friends quickly grew into a religious community where queer people, their families, and our allies could commune as equals in God's love. CAC became an antidote to the religious hatred we'd experienced, a safe space where religion meant peace, love, unity, equality, and justice for all.

When Uganda's Anti-Homosexuality Act was signed into law in February 2014, queer Ugandans started fleeing from violence and arbitrary arrest into Kenya. CAC was there to welcome and link arriving refugees and asylum seekers with organisations that could provide support. Offering these services and a new spiritual home for our Ugandan siblings brought new energy and life to the fellowship. It also gave CAC a clearer mission.

CAC now exists to affirm what's always been true: we are worthy of love, we deserve dignity, we are enough. Through fellowship, our members have found the strength to finally believe these truths. We host weekly worship experiences every Sunday in Kisumu and Nairobi. We also organise artistic performances, picnics, hiking, and camping trips to share these affirmations and build our community.

As we reclaim religion as a source of empowerment and liberation, we also combat religiously driven violence against our communities by engaging with grassroots faith and community leaders and working with the media to tell our stories.

These outreach efforts helped us establish the United Coalition of Affirming Africans, which works to advance the rights of sexual and gender minorities and create more LGBTIQ-affirming faith communities across the continent.

What started as hopes and dreams among queer friends has blossomed into a family, a community, a movement. Our doors and hearts are open to anyone in search of a safe space to experience the abundance of God's creativity, diversity, and love.

Just knock and you can enter.

David Ochara is a co-founder and ordained minister at Cosmopolitan Affirming Community (CAC) in Kenya.

WACØM
BOY

THINKING FOR MYSELF, FIGHTING FOR OUR COMMUNITY

BULELANI MZILA
South Africa

I was born in a mud house to a domestic worker and a gardener. It was Pietermaritzburg, 1989. South African history tells us it was the peak of Black-on-Black violence, the dawn of democracy. I was too young to remember apartheid but old enough to experience it. The evil system deprived Black people of opportunities. We're still feeling its legacy today.

At six years old I was confronted with the concepts of gender and sexuality for the first time. We were playing games after school when one of my classmates asked if I was a girl or a boy. "I'm a boy," I responded. They didn't believe me. The other kids teased my "girly" behaviour and told me I wasn't a "normal boy." A "stabane," they called me, an anti-queer slur that stabbed through my heart.

From that day forward I knew I was different from other kids. The bullying hurt, but it helped me understand that gender is a social construct. People try to change you, to turn you into something or someone you're not, to force you to fit their idea of what's "right," even if it feels wrong. What could I do?

At 10 I moved from Pietermaritzburg to live with my aunt in Soweto. Space was tight, so we slept on the floor. Around that time South African entertainer Somizi Mhlongo came out as gay on national television and started hosting a talk show in drag. I remember hearing hushed rumours

Illustration by Khanya Kemani

that the kwaito singer Lebo Mathosa was bisexual. These stories were taboo in my community, giggled or whispered around me, but they revealed an important truth. People like me existed.

A few years later, just as I was settling into high school, I lost my mother. She was HIV-positive and died from pneumonia. Mired in grief and with no one to talk to, I started questioning things. Why her? Why this? Why now? Mom died just when I was coming of age. Her own mother died when she was 16, forcing her to drop out of school to work and raise her siblings. She spent her entire life providing. To me she was the epitome of gender-nonconforming — she was my mom and my dad. As her gender-nonconforming child, I wanted to make her proud.

When it came time to choose a subject for Grade 10, I chose history. I thought studying the past would help me escape my present, but then I read a quote that sparked a dream: "If you do not think about politics, politics will think for you." This idea stuck with me. I couldn't shake it. It pushed me to question politicians and their power, to hold parties accountable, and to play my part in protecting our young democracy.

From then on I knew I wanted to become a politician, but daily hardships squashed my dream. Right after high school, I became homeless. I lost all hope and confidence. I was just living to survive to the next day.

At 22 I tested HIV-positive. I imagined death, but then I came across the National LGBTI Health Campaign and enrolled in their HIV/AIDS training programme. I learned that I could still lead a long and healthy life. I decided to move back to KZN for a fresh start and to put things in perspective.

The first six months were hard. I couldn't find a job, so I volunteered with the Gay & Lesbian Network in Pietermaritzburg and completed a certified HIV/AIDS counselling course. These skills helped me land a job with Community Media Trust, and soon I was presenting and co-hosting shows on a local radio station. Friends around me were addicted to ecstasy and alcohol, but I was focused on changing my life for the better.

My dream of joining politics slowly came back to me, but I didn't see anyone like me, any members of our local LGBTQI+ community, involved. Pietermaritzburg is small, and I often felt unsafe and unable to express myself, but I knew our voices needed to be heard. When I came across a fellowship programme that promised to train queer South African political activists, I remembered that quote, "If you do not think about politics, politics will think for you." I jumped at the opportunity and was selected to join the network.

Since that training in 2019, I've never looked back. LGBTQI+ people need political representation, and we need to exercise our political voice. COVID lockdowns have only emphasised the intense discrimination, marginalisation, hate crimes, and political exclusion our queer communities face.

That's why I launched the Isibani Civil Society Forum in 2020. The Forum seeks to engage political parties and the government to amplify political participation and inclusion of LGBTQI+ people and promote inclusive government policy on issues like gender-affirming health care. By coming together as one community, I believe we can amplify our voices and achieve political liberation.

The Isibani Civil Society Forum has shown me the importance of engaging political parties. As an active member of the African National Congress in my ward, I continue to face heteronormative and patriarchal biases. Rather than shy away, I now confront these biases head-on because I know I represent our queer community. One day I hope to represent all communities as an elected member of the KZN Legislature.

I'm still thinking about politics and thinking for myself, but thinking only gets you so far. I'm now working hard to raise queer voices and fighting for the political representation we deserve.

Bulelani Mzila is a political activist and founder of the Isibani Civil Society Forum in Pietermaritzburg, South Africa.

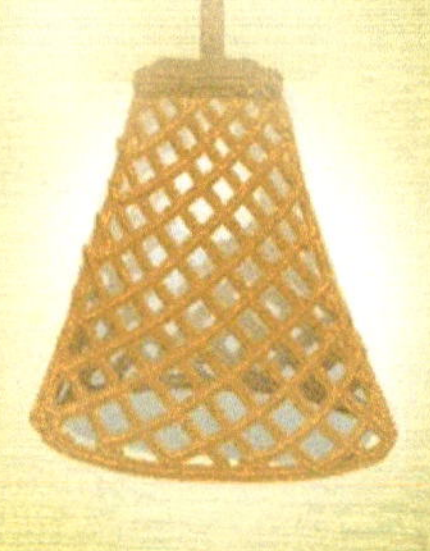

Mercy Thokozane Minah

BUILDING A BODY, TELLING OUR STORY

PAMINA SEBASTIÃO
Angola

I write and rewrite this, trying to sound less vulnerable. But why? Vulnerability should be part of our activism. How else can we grow and reflect?

For many years, I was my activism. I was raised in Angola and Portugal steeped in social justice. My sister and I were privileged to grow up in a home that valued education and exposed us to stories of change. My only path forward was a life of social and political transformation.

I started this journey by volunteering with artistic projects that created new forms of activism. It was fascinating to see people I respect transform their ideas into concrete action.

I had ideas, but I also had doubts. Could I create something meaningful on my own?

The short answer is no. None of us can. It took me years to realise that our colonial model of activism that centres singular activists as heroes of their own narratives was tearing us apart. These "founder" myths are competitive traps that feed the lie that one "star activist" working in isolation can build an empire. I wanted to build a collective, an LBTIQ feminist collective. In a collective, there can be no singular hero or protagonist. This is our story.

Illustration by Mercy Thokozane Minah

What's now called Arquivo de Identidade Angolano (AIA) started around an old table in my family's living room in 2016. My sister and I both identify as bisexual women and were both members of Angola's first LGBTIQ organisation, Iris. One day some friends came over and we started discussing how we could create something new. We all wanted to build a space where we could evolve, adapt, and imagine new beginnings. We wanted to show our conservative society and the world that queer Angolans exist.

In the years that followed, we created LGBTIQ video testimonies, translated queer rights resources into Portuguese, and documented our journey in a blog. Our growing archive linked past stories to present selves. We became part of an African movement to tell and preserve queer stories, writing our existence into history. We also became a feminist collective, our website serving as an intersectional political space where our bodies could be seen.

It was clear to us that feminism and LGBTIQ rights were part of the same political transformation we hoped to achieve, but not everyone could see this bridge. Much of the LGBTIQ community viewed feminists as radical and insensitive "man-eaters," and few LBTIQ women considered themselves feminists. By linking feminist principles to our queer bodies and the content we created for AIA, we found our intersectional fight.

Exploring different representations of our intersectional identities allowed us to create a new movement, but it also divided our bodies into fragments. We faced highs and lows, emotional violence, and constant burnout, but at least we still had homes.

The same wasn't true for Marcelo, a teenager who came to us for help after his family rejected him for being gay.

As Marcelo slept on my old sofa I would call his family and try to convince them to take him back, all the while wondering if this was even wise. Marcelo and other queer people who came to our doorstep needed a safe space where they could live freely. They needed families who love them for who they are. They needed a nurturing community. They needed a home.

AIA built No Cubico in 2017 as an LGBTQI safe space for cultural and educational activities. When we entered our new office and home for the first time, we knew that every person who walked through those doors would be okay. No Cubico quickly evolved into a shelter, some nights hosting 10 or more people. Reimagining and redefining what AIA could be made our safe space come alive. It's what made this a collective journey.

Our collective continues to thrive for one important reason: it's always been bigger than its founders. As people come and go, AIA evolves to meet the community's needs, with each of us playing an integral role in advancing the movement. Everyone has a voice. Everyone contributes. Everyone benefits.

AIA is living proof that real change comes when people work together. I'm so proud of what we've built.

Pamina would like to thank Kamy, Rosie, Liria, Leopoldina, Joana, Igor, Erickson, Jazmine, all volunteers at the shelter, everyone who has donated money, books, furniture, and clothes, everyone who has helped produce videos, photos, and AIA's website, and everyone who has provided emotional and intellectual support through the years.

Pamina Sebastião is an "artivist" and a co-founder of Arquivo de Identidade Angolano (AIA) in Luanda, Angola.

BLOOMING
QUEER

SIX TIMES TOO MANY

BAKANG NDABA
Botswana

By 15 I had already attempted suicide not once, not twice, but six times.

I was a queer boy in Botswana growing up in a traditional, conservative family that feared change. A family that didn't see sexual and gender minorities as human beings. A family that forced me to pretend everything was fine and to follow the path they had set for me without questioning where it would lead.

All I had were questions.

Where do I stand? Who can I trust? How should I behave?

Why is this happening? What's wrong with me? When will I be free?

I always knew I was different. I was the boy who crushed on other boys. I knew no one like me, no one to tell me that my desire wasn't a disease or a demon, no one to calm my nerves.

My reality. This thing. What was this thing? It was an "abomination," a "sin," a "phase." Was it a joke? No child in my family could actually be gay. I had watched my aunt chase her daughters away because they fell pregnant out of wedlock before finishing school. They messed up, so they faced the consequences. I learned their lessons. I couldn't mess up.

And so I was the perfect child. Or at least I tried to be. For a time. For as long as I could bear it.

Illustration by Lame Dilotsotlhe

When I couldn't take it anymore, I tried suicide.

Each attempt to end my life failed. When I tried to drown myself in the bathtub, I came up gasping for air. Fate had other plans. So I found other ways of "coping." I started self-harming, but that only made things worse. When classmates saw the scars on my arms and legs they called me a Satanist. They said I drank my own blood. This was my life. This is what I amounted to.

At 17, after trying and failing to accept my sexuality for years, I met a peer educator on Facebook who invited me to a support group for queer and questioning youth in Botswana. The group helped me understand my sexuality and see that I'm not alone in this world.

The emotional burden that had cut me, that had nearly drowned me, started to lift. For the first time in my life I felt like I belonged, like I wasn't an outcast. I felt free. I wanted to help other young people discover this sense of freedom, to understand that it's okay to be gay, to be androgynous, to be who you are and to embrace an identity beyond heteronormative expectations and structures.

That's when I became an activist. In 2018 I started a movement called PrEP Squad BW, an online safe space where young people in Botswana can find information about HIV/AIDS and prevention, explore their genders and sexualities, and receive free online counselling. Since launching, we've helped around 50 young Batswana access STI screening services and medication to prevent HIV infection. This work showed me how important public health programming is for our community, but I knew I could do more.

I joined Success Capital as a steering committee member and research consultant to engage more directly in civic action. Success Capital is a local LGBTIQ+ organisation that empowers queer youth and prepares them to thrive in the job market. We also lobby high-level policymakers to serve diverse marginalised groups and address our needs.

When Botswana's High Court decriminalised same-sex sexual activity in 2019, I could see the positive impact PrEP Squad BW, Success Capital, and other queer-centred organisations and initiatives were having on our community. We could finally love who we love without fear of arrest. "Discrimination has no place in this world. All human beings are born equal," Judge Leburu said when delivering the decrim ruling, but not all Batswana agreed.

As queer communities and allies around the world celebrated our victory, homophobic hate speech and attacks spiked online. The progress we achieved in court met resistance in the public square. This backlash resurfaced the trauma of our youth — the shaming, the othering, the discrimination — but it also inspired us to keep teaching people what they don't understand about our diversity, our humanity, our equality.

That's when I decided to visit my conservative family. I went to my mother first.

When I came out to her, she was lost for words. She feared change, but she also feared losing me. Over time, bit by bit, she's come to acknowledge and accept my truth.

Six times I tried to kill myself. I kiss the ground for each time I failed. Although my suicidal thoughts have retreated, I still keep close tabs on my mental health. When childhood traumas creep up, I remember how far I've come, all the progress we've made, all the allies fighting by our sides. Six times was six times too many. I won't make it seven.

Bakang Ndaba is a Motswana activist, poet, debater, feminist, and student who works to promote sexual and reproductive health and rights in Botswana.

why why why
why why why
why why why why

THE POWER OF "WHY?"

TIMIEBI EBITIBITUWA
Nigeria

I was the little girl who asked "why?"

I asked innocent questions to understand the world. I asked provocative questions to make people think. I asked uncomfortable questions to challenge the status quo. I asked probing questions to expose wrongs.

My questions had consequences.

Asking questions is a clever way to speak up for what you believe in and stand up for people whose questions often go unanswered or ignored. Does that make me an activist? I suppose it does.

As a millennial growing up in western Nigeria, words like "diversity," "tolerance," and "human rights" were never part of daily conversation.

I was told that people from different tribes were shady and that my religion was supreme. There was never much discussion about treating others with dignity and respect. We were expected to observe, assimilate, and replicate how "people like us" behaved.

Don't ask why. Toe the line. You'll be fine...unless you're different. Unless you're queer.

Blindly following existing attitudes is precisely how homophobia, transphobia, and violence against LGBTQI+ people seep from one

Illustration by Annabela Bekker

generation to the next. I only realised this when I moved to the U.K. in 2010. Living in a society where questions are encouraged opened my eyes. I was free to ask "why?" without someone accusing me of rebelling against my culture or undermining some sacred belief. London seemed like a magical place where people lived authentically and loved who they loved without fearing a death sentence.

The U.K. offered a painful contrast to Nigeria, where LGBTQI+ people's rights and freedoms were regularly trampled upon by government officials who are supposed to protect all citizens.

Things got worse in 2014 when Nigeria's Same Sex Marriage (Prohibition) Act became law. The new law went far beyond regulating marriage and sex, making it illegal to formally register or join an LGBTQI+ organisation. It was a devastating blow that gave Nigerian society free rein to discriminate against queer people. I watched in horror as anti-queer attacks and homophobic violence rose. I felt helpless.

I left the U.K. and moved back to Nigeria in 2016 determined to make a positive difference. LGBTQI+ equality seemed like an impossible goal, so I started small, using my social networks and social media platforms to call out homophobia and challenge people to interrogate their own biases against sexual and gender minorities.

I soon started working with The Initiative for Equal Rights (TIERs), Nigeria's leading LGBTQI+ civil society organisation, to create public advocacy messages around gender equality, sexual diversity, transphobia, and being an ally. These campaigns linked me with grassroots activists who work tirelessly to protect the human rights of LGBTQI+ people across the country. Their bravery inspired me and strengthened my commitment to the cause.

Although I don't personally identify as queer, I knew my voice mattered in this conversation. I knew I could use my words to change narratives and perspectives; to challenge Nigerian society to acknowledge queer people's humanity and affirm their right to equality, dignity, and respect. I also knew it wouldn't be easy.

One day I was walking home through Adekunle Ajasin University in Ondo State, South West Nigeria when I looked up and saw a billboard that read, "Stop dressing to provoke sexual harassment." The enormous sign blamed sexual harassment on women who wear "dresses that expose their bodies."

I was livid. I took a photo of the sign and posted it on Twitter with the caption: "We will not progress with the fight against sexual harassment as long as dutty stinking narratives like this continue to exist!" My tweet went viral and someone created a petition calling on the university to remove the billboard. Less than 24 hours later, it was gone.

If my words could bring such rapid change on behalf of women's dignity, I knew they could do the same for sexual and gender minorities. It would just take more time.

In 2020 I started working as communications and content officer for the International Centre for Advocacy on Rights to Health (ICARH). ICARH provides human rights and paralegal services to ensure the promotion and protection of the rights of sexual minorities and people living with HIV/AIDS in Nigeria. At ICARH I've found a home and a platform to help amplify LGBTQI+ voices.

The little girl who asked "why?" is still inside me. She paved the way for the fearless woman I've become. She's still asking "why?" but she's no longer asking for change. Now she's demanding it.

Timiebi Ebitibituwa is communications and content officer at the International Centre for Advocacy on Rights to Health (ICARH) in Abuja, Nigeria.

T·A·K·A

OUR FIGHT HAS ONLY JUST BEGUN

DAVID LARBI
Ghana

We struggle to survive from the moment we're born. For some of us, that struggle feels more like a war.

I grew up in Ghana with a toxic family and no support system. I couldn't afford basic materials for school, but I knew I needed to finish my studies. I had dreams. I had grit. I'd do anything to survive. And so I graduated.

That battle prepared me for my next calling — queer activism and community building in a country that fights our very right to exist.

In January 2021, our organisation LGBT+ Rights Ghana opened the nation's first queer community centre in Accra. We held a beautiful housewarming ceremony with live music under rainbow umbrellas and flags. We cut ribbons. We celebrated. We were open. And then we were closed.

What else could we do? Almost immediately we were overwhelmed by hate speech and death threats. Journalists and lawmakers discussed the "cult of homosexuality" as a "foreign import" and said we were "initiating" people at our new community space. They said we promote "moral decadence" and represent a "curse on the nation." Other false rumours spread like wildfire. Caught in this crusade, our safe space wasn't safe, so we shut it down.

Illustration by Larissa (Lari) Mwanyama

I felt ashamed — not for myself or my queer community, but for my country. This homophobic uproar showed the world what we've always known is true, that Ghana promotes hate speech, rape culture, victim-blaming, and violence towards its most marginalised citizens.

Too many Ghanaians believe God will unleash his wrath if queer people achieve the most basic rights. These are the same people who paradoxically argue that part of what made Ghana glorious before colonialism was a stronger sense of unity in diversity. Pre-colonial society was indeed more tolerant of sexual and gender diversity than what we see today, but artificial land borders have cut into relationships and identities. Foreign religions have brought unrealistic demands.

In Ghana today, diversity is abhorred. Sermons that bash queer people are considered "uplifting." Preachers pluck isolated verses from the Bible to ostracise us. Imams make it nearly impossible for us or even our allies to live in Muslim communities. We're being blackmailed, extorted, lynched, and publicly humiliated while community leaders watch from the sidelines or stoke the flames.

After 64 years of independence, Ghanaians now lag further behind in our perceptions of progress than when we started. Marginalised groups like the LGBT+ community have made little headway in our fight for equality. Our sensitisation and education campaigns can only accomplish so much when well-financed religious and political organisations fight tooth and nail to oppose our every move.

And yet, we're still fighting.

LGBT+ Rights Ghana started in 2018 as a cyber activism blog to tell the world what was happening to us. Since then we've spearheaded new initiatives to strengthen and support our community.

"Here & Beyond" brings queer people together each month to socialise, network, and build the movement. "Community Studio Discussion" offers an online safe space where LGBT+ people can share personal stories and discuss how to overcome internalised homophobia, combat discrimination and violence, and use the law to advocate for our community's interests. The "Ghana Gay Blackmail List" lets LGBT+ people report abuse and expose people who con or extort us.

In 2019 LGBT+ Rights Ghana pushed back against the World Congress of Families (WCF), a U.S.-based anti-LGBT+ hate group, when it hosted a regional gathering in Accra. We mobilised ally organisations and individuals to condemn the conference and registered members to attend and document WCF's strategies so that we can better counter them.

We're now working to become Ghana's first group formally registered as an LGBT+ organisation. We believe this visibility will help counter the misuse of culture, tradition, and religious conservatism to silence sexual and gender minorities.

Our guiding principles at LGBT+ Rights Ghana are inclusivity, integrity, solidarity, and accountability. We're working hard to build a Ghana where the rights of LGBT+ persons are respected and protected.

Our community centre is closed for now, but it won't be closed forever. Our fight for equality has only just begun.

David Larbi is a founding member and the general secretary of LGBT+ Rights Ghana in Accra.

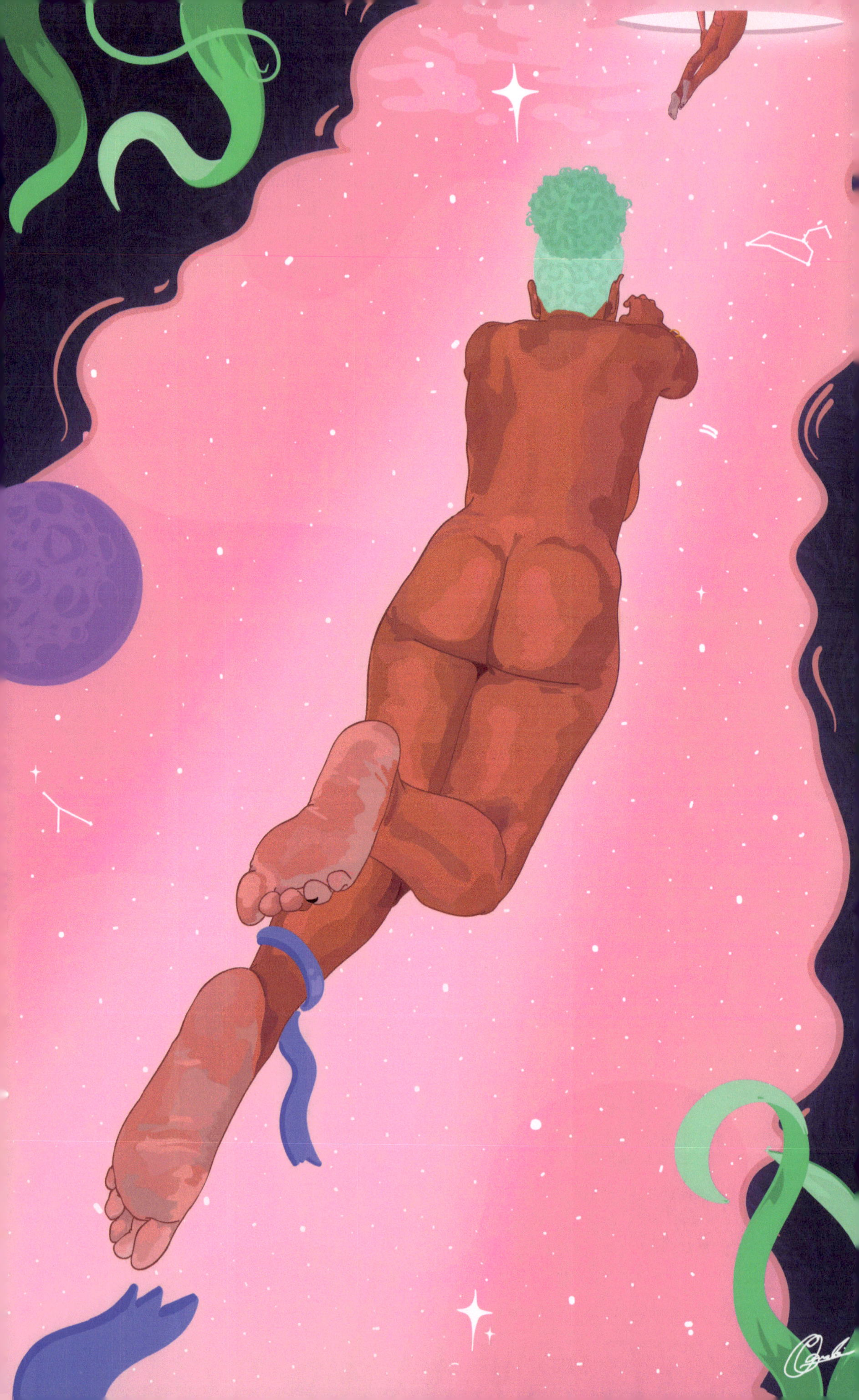

Queer Privilege

A POEM BY "MYSTIQUE"

Queer privilege is sitting through a church sermon listening
To the preacher talk about abominations, sins of the flesh, demons,
And convincing you your place is in Hell right next to the devil.
It is being told to dress more feminine if you want to come to church,
Ignoring the fact that you don't identify as a woman.
Queer privilege is dreading the "when are you getting married?" conversations
That come with every family gathering.
It's knowing you will never have the chance to introduce the love of your life
To your mother or take things to the next level.
Queer privilege is that voice in the back of your head that keeps screaming
"What if they are right?"
It's depression, self-doubt, self-hatred, and suicidal thoughts.
Queer privilege is having to change the pronouns in all your love poems
Right before you perform them.
It's not being able to hold hands in public places or go on dates.
Queer privilege is being a sunflower without the sun, constantly hiding in the shadow
So they don't crush and grind you.
It's being stuck in a closet even though you suffer from claustrophobia.

Illustration by Lamb of Lemila

"Mystique" is a spoken word artist. Their work addresses social ills around religion, gender, sexual orientation, and politics. Their art aims to spark conversations on topics that are usually silenced in mainstream discourse.

LGBTQI+
NEWS Phebean Swill
LEGAL
DELL
Mercy Thokozane Minah

NEVER GIVE UP. YOU WILL MAKE IT!

JENNEH MUSTAPHA
Sierra Leone

When did I know? I knew I wanted to be a journalist at 15 after hearing an episode of the talk show *Wake Up Sierra Leone*. I'll never forget it.

It was 2006, and that morning's featured guest was a local politician. He said most girls who play sports are lesbians. He called on the government to kill LGBTQI+ people. I was horrified. He was talking about me.

The host that morning was a young journalist named Phebean Swill. She challenged the guest's dangerous homophobia and spoke out on our behalf. From that moment I admired Phebean and all journalists who stand up for LGBTQI+ people, especially in a country as difficult as mine.

Being queer in Sierra Leone is an affront to our culture and traditions, people say. "It's a Western import." "We do it for money." "It doesn't exist." These are lies. Lies that deny our humanity. Lies that restrict our human rights.

I was 10 when I realised I was attracted to other girls. "Don't you have a boyfriend?" my mother asked a few years later. I lied and said I did, but the pressure kept mounting.

Mum and other family members ridiculed me for being a tomboy. "Your cousins keep giving birth, what are you waiting for?" they asked more frequently the older I got. They knew about my sexuality. They must have known. But they didn't accept it.

Illustration by Mercy Thokozane Minah

I left home to stay with friends, but discrimination and hate speech followed. People didn't understand me. They wanted to shut me up. I refused to fall silent.

My first job after university was as a communications assistant for the Red Cross. It wasn't journalism exactly, but it involved similar skills. The West African Ebola outbreak was in full swing, and we were bombarded with requests from journalists who were working hard to keep the public safe and informed. One day I noticed a familiar face. It was Phebean.

I was so excited to meet one of my idols. I told her how moved I was by that interview she'd done so many years ago defending LGBTQI+ people, defending us. I told her I wanted to learn from her expertise and become a powerful journalist like her. So Phebean became my mentor.

She taught me how to edit news videos and create documentaries, and I kept her informed about our work at the Red Cross. Our professional relationship quickly developed into something more. Phebean became my friend. She became my rock.

After two years working for the Red Cross, I lost my job because of my sexuality. My supervisor was jealous of the attention and respect I received from donors and higher-ups and told his brother, the head of Sierra Leone Red Cross Society, that I date men and women. Two months later I was fired due to "funding cuts."

I was devastated, but Phebean was there again to give me hope. "Never give up. You will make it," she told me. Two years passed without work. I volunteered as a camera operator at a local television station, but I needed a job that paid. I repeated Phebean's words over and over. "Never give up. You will make it." These words became my mantra. And then they came true.

One day I attended a training on LGBTQI+ safety and security hosted by the Concerned Women's Initiative of Sierra Leone, a lesbian-led organisation. At the workshop I met the executive director of the Lesbian and Gay Association of Liberia (LEGAL) and told her my story. She asked me if I wanted to work with them in Liberia as LEGAL's programmes and communications manager. I jumped at the opportunity and moved to Monrovia.

Our mission at LEGAL is to advocate for the rights of LGBTQI+ people, with a particular focus on access to social justice and healthcare services. It's a tough job. Some people harass us with hate speech. Some refuse to work with us because of who we represent. Whenever I feel discouraged, I remember the mantra Phebean gifted me.

Although I'm in Liberia now and Phebean is in Sierra Leone, we still video chat most days. She's still my idol, my mentor, my friend. As a queer teenager coming to terms with my gender and sexuality, she publicly defended the humanity of LGBTQI+ people and gave us strength. As a young adult in crisis, she gave me hope. With allies like Phebean by our side, queer people like me will never give up.

We will make it.

Jenneh Mustapha is programmes and communications manager at the Lesbian and Gay Association of Liberia (LEGAL) in Monrovia.

OUR
ARE
FOR
CHANGE
naija
VOICE
things
LGBT+

OUR VOICES ARE CALLING FOR CHANGE

MIKE DAEMON
Nigeria

When I first started the NoStringsNG podcast, I didn't know what I was doing. I just wanted the world to hear me, to know that I — a gay man in Nigeria — exist.

Growing up gay in this heteronormative and homophobic country was hellish. I had to hide my sexuality from everyone. People who suspected my truth called me all sorts of names. I was bullied for associating with effeminate boys. At one point, I was beaten on my way home from school. I was terribly injured but couldn't tell anyone why. I stayed silent to stay safe.

As a young man, I battled with depression. I felt insignificant and lost. I withdrew from society and into myself. Eventually, in this isolation, I somehow found my voice. I realised I wasn't actually alone. There were other young men like me facing the same doubts, the same loneliness, the same rejection. I wanted to tell them they mattered. Our voices needed to be heard.

Illustration by Amina Gimba

I recorded the first episode of NoStringsNG from a mattress on my mother's floor. The sound quality wasn't great, but I didn't care. I only cared about telling my story. That first episode explored homophobia, bullying, and self-acceptance. My goal was to inspire other queer people going through similar situations not to lose hope. I uploaded the audio file and hit publish.

That was seven years ago. What started with a cheap microphone on my home computer has since grown into Nigeria's premier LGBT+ media advocacy organisation. Today our platforms and initiatives help thousands of queer Nigerians tell their stories to audiences around the world.

NoStringsNG uses the power of storytelling to dismantle dangerous myths and misconceptions about sexual and gender diversity. One falsehood many Nigerians believe is that HIV is a "gay disease." To counter this lie, we invited a young man living with HIV to speak about his experience on the podcast. This in-depth fact-based conversation helped listeners understand the science behind HIV transmission and prevention and how stigma harms LGBT+ persons' mental health and worsens the discrimination they face. Another podcast episode explored family rejection, a major problem affecting queer communities in Nigeria and globally. That episode offered advice about coming out and addressed some of the questions and fears many parents face when queer children disclose their identities.

As a media group, NoStringsNG is constantly developing innovative strategies and new technologies to solve issues that plague the queer community. Our latest addition is Qtalk, a social and counselling mobile app that connects LGBT+ Nigerians to volunteer doctors and therapists who provide free psychosocial and legal support. The app also serves as a platform for queer people to share their struggles and form meaningful friendships. Launched in March 2020, QTalk is already making a difference.

In Port Harcourt, a trans woman who was evicted from home after her landlord learned about her gender identity was able to access support from a counsellor who connected her to a local trans group that provides safe emergency shelter. In Lagos, a young gay man who was bullied at school sought support on QTalk and was connected to an LGBT+ organisation that helped him overcome the harassment. These and countless other success stories inspire us to expand.

In 2019 we co-founded the African Human Rights Media Network (AHRMN) to broaden our impact. This coalition of activists and journalists uses members' websites and social media platforms to amplify LGBT+ voices in Africa, helping us reach more people than ever before.

We're also taking direct action. Near the end of 2020, NoStringsNG used its vast network to rally support for queer Nigerians impacted by the COVID-19 pandemic. We collected donations from generous individuals around the world and distributed emergency supplies and financial support to hundreds of LGBT+ Nigerians across the country.

This work fills me with so much hope for the future. I can see that we're improving queer Nigerians' lives and changing mindsets. We're giving voice to the voiceless and showing the world we exist. That's all I wanted when I started NoStringsNG, but now I know it's not enough.

We need tolerance, acceptance, equality. Our voices are calling for change.

Mike Daemon is the founder of NoStrings Development Initiatives, a Nigeria-based non-profit organisation that works to promote and amplify the voices and visibility of LGBT+ Nigerians.

THE PROMISE OF HOPE

KASHINDI SHABANI GADY
Democratic Republic of the Congo

In early 2019, a crowd of 1,000 people burned tyres outside Bukavu's city hall to protest against our LGBTI community. "Go into their homes, burn them down," one man shouted through a megaphone.

The mob gathered after posters started appearing around town calling for homosexuality and gender diversity to be criminalised. The man behind the posters was a local pastor who regularly tells congregants and his radio show audience that LGBTI people should be kicked out of the country.

There are no specific laws against being LGBTI in the Democratic Republic of the Congo, but there's plenty of hatred.

Our human rights are violated every day. We face arbitrary arrest for illegitimate offences, rejection from our families and society, discrimination in employment and education, inadequate healthcare, so-called "corrective" rape, and other forms of violence.

The persecution is relentless.

The dangers we face are so extreme that many LGBTI people are scared to leave wherever they call home. For some, home is five people living in a tiny room, forced together to survive after being shunned by their families or evicted by bigoted landlords.

Illustration by Annabela Bekker

For many queer people in the DRC, life is misery. There's no money because there's no work, which means there's no food. Many of us survive by begging in the street or taking up sex work.

In 1998 I fled the DRC and sought asylum in Ireland. There I worked with several NGOs and learned how to support vulnerable populations in exercising their human rights to healthcare, security, shelter, and emotional support.

My two decades in Ireland were incredibly rich, but I knew my community needed me back home, especially after the DRC government tried to criminalise homosexuality in 2016. Homophobic and transphobic rhetoric and attacks were on the rise and getting worse.

I returned to Bukavu in 2017 and co-founded Savie Asbl, an NGO that fights anti-queer hatred and works to increase the number of workplaces in the DRC that are LGBTI-inclusive. We also help sexual and gender minorities access healthcare and education.

Since the COVID-19 pandemic arrived here in 2020, life in the DRC has become more difficult for everyone. Queer people have been especially hard hit.

Lockdown measures forced many LGBTI people to self-isolate in hostile and queerphobic environments with unsupportive family members or co-habitants. Although most of us are no longer self-isolating, I speak with people every day who are still trapped in these terrible conditions.

The pandemic and ensuing lockdowns continue to have devastating impacts on the livelihoods and healthcare needs of LGBTI people. At Savie Asbl we are working to address a range of community needs, including the provision of emergency food and shelter, access to safe and competent healthcare, and financial stability.

It's been a tough few years for our community. Savie Asbl is doing its best to bring hope during these grim times and to create a brighter, more inclusive, more equitable future for LGBTI people to enjoy when the pandemic finally lifts.

Kashindi Shabani Gady is the executive secretary of Savie Asbl NGO PGEL LGBTI DRC in Bukavu, Democratic Republic of the Congo.

My God is Queer

A POEM BY "MYSTIQUE"

"We are all made in the image of the Lord"
To me, this means the way you see yourself is the way your God will be shaped
So when you preach hate in his name
It is because you yourself are full of hatred
When you preach exclusion
It's coming from your exclusionary nature
When you use his name to justify homophobia
It is because you are homophobic
So don't tell me "God does not like queer people"
Don't tell me that queer love is a sin in his eyes
Don't tell me queerness is a demon to be exorcised
Because that is not my God
That is your God
My God is non-binary
That is why he could make both man and woman in his image
My God is a Lesbian
That is why the most beautiful wedding vows are those spoken by Ruth to Naomi
My God is Gay
That is why he poured abundant blessings upon King David
My God is Bisexual
My God is Trans
My God is Intersex
My God is Queer
My God is Love

"Mystique" is a spoken word artist. Their work addresses social ills around religion, gender, sexual orientation, and politics. Their art aims to spark conversations on topics that are usually silenced in mainstream discourse.

WACOM BOY

A FUTURE WHERE QUEER LOVE CAN BLOOM

FRANK LILEZA
Mozambique

I am a young and empowered Mozambican man. I love art and soul music. I am inspired by nature and the telling of real-life stories.

Hundreds of people share these same qualities, but I'm unique: I'm gay and non-binary.

I came out of the closet to three close friends when I turned 17. It was an ordinary day after school. We were all at my friend Thandy's house for our usual tea time.

I was talking a lot. I was nervous. I worried about how they would react. I didn't know if they would continue to be my friends after learning my truth.

Fortunately, my fears came to naught. My friends were wonderful. Nothing changed between us. At last, I could be the real me. Or so I thought.

Two years later at university, I fell in love for the first time with a man from my class. He was tall and skinny, a man with kind eyes and a generous soul. It was a beautiful experience to be in love with someone and to feel those sensations. I had never felt that way for anyone; my heart finally received something that for many years it had cried for.

I still cry looking back.

Illustration by Khanya Kemani

My first love came at the wrong time. It was secret. It was forbidden. LGBT issues were not even discussed in Mozambique. Although our love was beautiful, it was also very confusing because of society's hyper-toxic masculinity that emphasises heterosexual relationships and traditional gender roles. As a non-binary gay man, where did I fit within this oppressive system? Our love never had a chance.

Even today I carry the marks of that first love. I still wonder, "what if?" What if we'd been able to express our love openly? What if society had accepted us? What if we hadn't needed to hide?

These questions pushed me to fight for LGBT equality. I couldn't sit idly by while more queer people were robbed of the chance to find great love and live openly.

In 2013 after finishing university I joined LAMBDA, Mozambique's leading organisation for the defence of sexual and gender minorities, as its public relations and communications specialist. I saw the job as an opportunity to join a cause that was also mine — to educate myself, to reinvent myself, to empower myself.

Now I work to protect the rights of LGBT people to be who we are, to live without fear.

Although we've been hampered by the government's 14-year denial of LAMBDA's petition to become a legally recognised association, we've always remained active in our fight for LGBT equality. A 2019 United Nations report praised LAMBDA's work, including our efforts lobbying the government to decriminalise homosexuality, which in 2015 was successful. We continue to provide safe spaces for LGBT communities as part of our larger mission to bring full human rights to all sexual and gender minorities.

No one should fear being openly LGBT the way I feared being open about my first love. LAMBDA's work helps me see a future without stigma and bias. A future where queer love can bloom.

Frank Lileza is a public relations and communications specialist at LAMBDA, Mozambique's leading LGBT rights organisation.

Dear Future Husband

A POEM BY "MYSTIQUE"

i promise to honour my wedding
vows
i will stand before the world and
profess
my willingness to spend forever with
you
Just so i can see a smile on my
mother's face

i promise i shall surrender my body
into your arms
And allow you to attempt to pleasure
it
And i will try to make sure it is your
face i see
When i cum, or at least pretend it is

i promise to bear and nurture
beautiful
Grandkids for our parents
i will make sure they always have a
good home
And parents that look and act happy

i promise to hold your hand in public
Gaze into your face with nothing but
respect
And adoration in my eye. To the
world, ours
Will be a picture-perfect union
i promise to be the wife that you
deserve
The one every man wishes he had
To always support and encourage you
Build an empire with you

Dear future husband
i promise you shall never know of the
loneliness
That fills my heart
The regret that lies deep within my
soul
Every time i think of the day i said
yes

i promise i will only shed tears of
sorrow
In your absence
Make sure you never have to see me
thinking
Of what could have been, but isn't

i promise i will try to love you at least
Half as much as I loved her

"Mystique" is a spoken word artist. Their work addresses social ills around religion, gender, sexual orientation, and politics. Their art aims to spark conversations on topics that are usually silenced in mainstream discourse.

activist

BEING AN ALLY MEANS SHOWING UP

SULEMANI MUHIRWA
Rwanda

I first heard about LGBTIQ Rwandans 20 years ago. I was in secondary school when a well-known Rwandan actor was attacked by a group of men over rumours the star was gay.

Sensational news of the attack spread as people gossiped, some labelling the celebrity evil, others calling for his death. My heart ached as I listened to him tearfully describe the assault during a radio interview. I couldn't understand why he'd been treated so terribly.

More than a decade later in 2014, I was hired at an NGO in Kigali that works with key populations across Rwanda. My main job was to link men who have sex with men (MSM), gay men, and transgender women with access to health services.

This was my first experience interacting with sexual and gender minorities and learning about their struggles. I came across several community organisations that promote healthcare access for key populations, but no one dared to talk about LGBTIQ equality. Cultural and religious beliefs fuelled too much bigotry and discrimination. Being queer was beyond taboo.

In one project, our NGO aimed to distribute health information to 300 MSM over three years. My boss warned me that because so many sexual minorities are closeted due to stigma, we might not reach our goal.

Illustration by Lame Dilotsotlhe

To encourage participation, I started meeting with the few LGBTIQ community leaders I could find to discuss the project's importance and goals. These activists enlightened me about the horrendous human rights violations sexual and gender minorities in Rwanda face.

I witnessed this anti-LGBTIQ bias and abuse first-hand. One health centre director in Kigali told me her facility would treat female sex workers but not MSM because she believed the latter group violate God's will and Rwandan cultural values.

A month later, when I invited LGBTIQ organisation leaders and members to come discuss the issues they face, almost 200 people showed up. This was the first time so many people in Rwanda had attended such an event.

In that meeting in Kigali, I promised LGBTIQ Rwandans that I am and will always be their ally. I empathised with the pain they felt when shunned by families and society. I offered my voice to help amplify the community's concerns and defend against human rights violations. I came ready to lose everything, including my reputation. In doing so, I became more than a public health worker. I became a human rights activist.

I gave my mobile number to everyone at the meeting and told them they could trust me. My phone rang day and night with calls from LGBTIQ people asking me to intervene in their struggles. I started following up on these cases of human rights violations and advocating for victims' rights.

At one point, my boss scolded me in front of other staff, saying I should focus on public health. LGBTIQ advocacy might hurt the reputation of our organisation, he said. I ignored his rebuke and started working closely with the LGBTIQ Coalition Isange Rwanda to develop advocacy strategies. This allowed me to facilitate meetings with law enforcement officials, media representatives, and social media influencers to advocate for change.

Over the years, I've been attacked and harassed for my advocacy of LGBTIQ equality. Once when I went to meet a police station commander on behalf of a trans woman who was arrested, the commander took me to a crowded area of the precinct and announced in a loud voice, "This man speaks for homosexuals." Immediately the crowd began shouting and mocking me. Some told the commander he should detain LGBTIQ people. Others shouted they should be killed.

I still face similar harassment, but it's never stopped me from advocating for the fair and equal treatment of LGBTQI people.

Seven years after I gave my phone number to that room of activists I continue to receive calls about LGBTIQ people who face human rights violations and discrimination. I'm still shocked to hear the lamentations of LGBTIQ Rwandans who have been chased from their families, to meet young trans women who are starving, to witness their rampant homelessness. I listen to them describe beatings, harassment, arrest, detention, and all forms of abuse.

I'm now one of the only people in Rwanda who speaks on live radio shows about the human rights violations LGBTIQ people face and their need for protection as equal members of our society. I've developed a thick skin after years of audience members phoning in to attack me for "promoting homosexuality."

Some friends say I'm an LGBTIQ ally because I'm secretly gay. Fellow congregants at my church have told me to quit advocating for the rights of queer people or God will punish us. I've learned to block out the gossip and hatred.

Being an ally to LGBTIQ people can be risky in hostile countries like Rwanda, but it's vital if you believe in equality, if you believe that everyone deserves dignity, love, and respect.

I promised to be an ally for life. I'm keeping my promise.

Sulemani Muhirwa is a public health expert, human rights activist, and volunteer policy adviser at Isange Rwanda, an LGBTIQ Coalition based in Kigali.

S+G

OVERCOMING ABUSE THROUGH "ARTIVISM"

STEPHEN OKWANY
Kenya

Drama Club was my hideout. Getting lost in a character helped me escape the terror of being a closeted bisexual at an all-boys high school. It taught me to act the way society expected me to act, to fly under the radar, to survive.

In my second year at Kisumu Boys High School in western Kenya, a gender non-binary boy named George joined the boarding wing after being outed as gay and expelled from their previous school. We played handball during games time and acted together on stage. Our affection for one another grew. We started dating. We did so secretly.

Our classmates were obsessed with outing sexual and gender minority students. After two academic terms, George was targeted by "Black Omena," a dreaded school gang that blackmailed queer students. The group included school staff, and our principal was a socially conservative priest, so there was little use in reporting their abuse to the administration.

We felt defenceless. We couldn't speak out.

For a long time, I hid my sexual orientation behind my large physique in order to escape the gang's humiliation and abuse. I worked out, flexed my muscles, and nobody discovered my secret. I was strong physically but hurt miserably inside.

Illustration by Neil Badenhorst

George had a harder time hiding their truth, so I became the strong one in our relationship. The struggle continued, but I kept protecting George from harm. Sometimes we would pay money to gang members in order to buy temporary immunity from harassment. All the while queer students around us were being outed, often publicly at social gatherings. I choked with fear.

Our only respite came on the occasional field trip to drama festivals. George and I would travel to other cities with the Drama Club, sometimes staying away together for up to two weeks. Because George boarded at the school and I was a day student, it was our only time alone together. I'd never been happier.

In our final year, I fell behind on my school payments so was unable to attend classes for several weeks. That meant I wasn't around to protect George.

One day during my absence, the Black Omena gang attacked George at a school sporting event. They body-shamed and humiliated George and pasted stories about them on a school notice board. George was traumatised, their self-esteem completely deflated.

When I came back to school, I found a broken George.

I was furious. I wanted revenge so badly, but speaking up would mean outing myself. I couldn't do it, and I didn't want to make things worse. I knew how awful George had it in the dormitories at night.

George couldn't take the attacks any longer. They faked an illness and went home to Kericho. That was the last time I ever saw or heard from George.

It broke me to pieces.

My academic performance deteriorated, but I still passed my exams. I was so relieved to be done with that school but still needed to return one more time to collect my certificate. That's when I met Kenny, who'd been hired to teach drama.

I saw Kenny leading a rehearsal and immediately loved her training techniques. She blended in well with the students, who never judged her non-binary gender expression. We became friends and she asked me to join her training team. She was busy working with the Kisumu Initiative for Positive Empowerment, a local LGBTQI+ rights group, and had less and less time to oversee rehearsals, so I started mentoring the drama students.

Kenny introduced me to "artivism," the concept of using the arts to achieve social change, and taught me how to write socially conscious scripts. The skills I gained working with Kenny gave me the confidence to establish Talanta Africa, an LGBTQI+ artivist organisation that uses art, media, culture, and technology to amplify queer voices in Kenya and beyond.

I'm using artivism to create a world where LGBTQI+ youth can self-explore and self-identify as they wish, where no one has to endure the mental, emotional, and physical abuse George and I suffered at school.

If George is still alive, I hope and pray they read my story and remember me fondly.

Stephen Okwany is an "artivist" whose passion lies in amplifying youth voices against violence and intimidation. He is the director of programmes at Talanta Africa.

GOD MADE US WHO WE'RE MEANT TO BE

UCHENNA SAMUEL NGENE
Nigeria

Gay. Christian. Nigerian. Man. People say my identities clash, but they're all I've ever known. These labels are pieces of my truth.

I was born and raised in southeastern Nigeria, the only child in a devout Catholic family. My parents taught me to fear God and love Jesus. I served the clergy at worship services and started evangelising for the Catholic Charismatic Renewal Movement before I was even a teenager.

In secondary school I started questioning my sexuality. I had always been effeminate and felt an innate attraction to other males from an early age. My first kiss was with a boy when I was nine years old. I knew what I felt, but I didn't have the words to describe it. "Gay" wasn't in my vocabulary yet.

I eventually learned what "gay" meant at church. Priests clobbered us with condemnation, preaching against homosexuality and other "sins." I believed what I heard — that my nature was sinful and repulsive.

I pored over scripture seeking alternative answers to this religious hatred. I was tired of suppressing my emotions, feelings, attractions, desires. I was tired of suppressing my truth. This questioning led me to Bible school and eventually to earn a university degree in philosophy and religion. It also helped me discover a thriving community of LGBTIQ Christians.

Illustration by Larissa (Lari) Mwanyama

In 2015 I started volunteering with House of Rainbow. House of Rainbow fosters relationships among LGBTIQ people of faith and their allies to create safer and more inclusive communities. Through this work I found support and eventually self-acceptance.

Reconciling my faith with my sexuality was an arduous journey. It led me to establish an organisation called Levites Initiative for Freedom and Enlightenment in 2016 to support other young Nigerian LGBTIQ people of faith in understanding and reconciling the pieces of their identities that society so often tears apart. Just like the Levites in the Bible helped protect and maintain sacred rituals and religious life at Jerusalem's ancient Temple, we support LGBTIQ people in practising their faith, so they feel included and loved.

At that point my own journey towards reconciliation was far from over. In 2017 I was expelled from singing in a Christian music group I loved because of the high visibility of my work challenging homophobic and heterosexist religious narratives. As one door closed, the right one opened. That same year I was elected as "Nigeria champion" at the Interfaith Diversity Network of West Africa (IDNOWA). IDNOWA dialogues with faith-based communities and implements education and advocacy programmes to foster self-acceptance.

I soon started collaborating with another group called Soulforce to create educational resources that debunk Christian queerphobia. Soulforce is a U.S.-based organisation that works to end the religious and political oppression of LGBTIQ people and heal their spirits. This led me to join The Reformation Project's leadership development programme, which aims to advance LGBTIQ inclusion in the Christian church.

In 2020 I joined the board of the Global Interfaith Network for People of all Sexes, Sexual Orientations, Gender Identities and Expressions. GIN-SSOGIE advocates for safe spaces, policy inclusion, and the support and acceptance of all sexual and gender minorities within faith communities. Through GIN-SSOGIE, I've highlighted the plight of LGBTIQ people of faith at high-level meetings and proposed collaborative advocacy reforms to improve our human rights.

As I reflect on where I've come from and what I've been through, I see that my journey has been marked by resilience. I've embraced my identities and challenged the status quo to uphold my personal truth. I care deeply about my relationship with God and now know that being who I am and being with who I love doesn't invalidate my faith.

I hope my journey of self-reconciliation offers a positive example for LGBTIQ people of faith to know that God's love is unconditional. As LGBTIQ people, our love is not a sin. God made us who we're meant to be.

Uchenna Samuel Ngene is the executive programmes director at Levites Initiative for Freedom and Enlightenment in Asaba, Nigeria.

POEMS
Mercy Thokozane Minah

CHIPPING AWAY AT INTOLERANCE

EPPY MUTETWA
Zimbabwe

Last year a friend and I decided to start a fitness journey together. Every morning we would wake up and walk around our neighbourhood in Harare. One day while we were stretching next to the road a young boy passed and rudely asked if we were both girls. "What do you think?" I asked with an awkward laugh. "That's a boy," he said pointing at my friend who was assigned female at birth, presents masculine, and uses they/them pronouns.

He spent the next three minutes invasively scrutinising my friend's chest while they did press-ups. "Haaaaa uyu musikana!" ("That's a girl!") he finally shouted with excitement. "Stop wearing male clothes and start wearing dresses," he added with a snarl. The nerve of this child. Where did he learn to behave?

Just then a group of men walked by. Rather than chastise the little boy, they shouted gross sexual comments at me and transphobic comments at my friend. We stopped exercising for a week and never returned to that spot where we were so harassed and humiliated.

To say this was an isolated incident would be a lie. Having queer friends in Zimbabwe means constantly witnessing the people you love get attacked by a society that refuses to embrace diversity.

When our late President Robert Mugabe uttered anti-gay statements at rallies or referred to sexual and gender diversity as "Western concepts"

Illustration by Mercy Thokozane Minah

designed to undermine "African morality," he planted seeds of hatred, intolerance, and discrimination in Zimbabweans young and old. I grew up seeing queerphobia normalised on the news but had never questioned it because I'd never felt its ugly claws in my heart.

That changed when I started university. I met my classmates with an open mind and soon found that some of my best friends were queer. The closer we grew, the harder it became for me to ignore homophobia and transphobia or pretend it didn't matter.

Every time we went out together my queer friends were harassed. I too was attacked. "You're too pretty to be hanging out with gay guys," strangers, usually straight men, would shout at me as we passed. Some assumed I was dating my masculine-presenting lesbian and non-binary friends and threatened to "cure" me with their penises. These men wanted to scare me into abandoning my queer friends. Weathering their disgusting assaults together only strengthened our bond.

During my third year at university, I took an internship helping to create sexual and reproductive health and rights resources for LGBTQ people. The gay men and trans women I interviewed told me shocking stories of the physical abuse, emotional torture, and so-called "corrective rape" they suffered at the hands of family members, church leaders, and law enforcement officials — the very people who should nurture and protect them.

These testimonies broke my heart, but they also opened my eyes to the gross human rights violations happening all around me. I decided enough was enough. I couldn't be a bystander or victim of this homophobic society any longer. It was time for me to stand up and do something, to help educate and inform people about sexual and gender diversity in my country.

My Body My Business: Digital Media Advocacy for the LGBTQ Community of Zimbabwe was my final year dissertation at university and the final push I needed to become an activist for LGBTQ equality. It took me three months to find a lecturer willing to supervise my topic. Most opposed it on moral or legal grounds, while others were afraid they would lose their jobs if they supervised me. The research process showed me how little academic research exists on LGBTQ identities in Africa. I came to realise this knowledge gap is what emboldens homophobic leaders to falsely dismiss sexual and gender diversity as "un-African." It also helps explain why African queer culture borrows so much from the West. These insights helped me see the value of documenting queer stories and experiences from an African perspective.

After finishing university in 2019, I started looking for volunteer and workshop opportunities with LGBTQ organisations in Zimbabwe. That's how I met Trevor Molife, founder and director of Purple Hand Africa, which advocates for and empowers LGBTQ people in Zimbabwe through mental wellness, livelihood, and skills training initiatives.

I joined Purple Hand Africa as project coordinator in 2019 and helped develop our Community Art Workshop model. This mental health initiative brings LGBTQ Zimbabweans together to express their challenges and triumphs using music, poetry, and creative writing as a means of advocacy. Last year we expanded on this initiative by producing a docuseries on mental health to keep queer Zimbabweans connected and motivated during COVID lockdowns.

We're still a long way from ending homophobia and transphobia in Zimbabwe, but I can already see the positive ways our initiatives are changing hearts and minds. We're chipping away at intolerance and building a society that values equality and respect. One day my queer friends and I will stop looking over our shoulders in fear and instead walk proudly with our heads held high. Until then, we'll keep celebrating our successes.

Eppy Mutetwa is programmes manager at Purple Hand Africa, an organisation that focuses on empowering Zimbabwe's LGBTQ community.

DK

PROUD TO BE DIFFERENT

DK DLAMINI
Eswatini

Growing up trans in Swaziland, I felt proud to be different. I flaunted it.

In primary school, I was suspended for refusing to wear the standard girls' uniform. My father pleaded with the headteacher to let me dress like the boys but to no avail. I settled on wearing tracksuits every day.

I always knew I was queer — my parents tried to raise me as a girl, and I knew I was attracted to girls — but I didn't know I was trans. How could I? I wasn't exposed to the right terminology and didn't know any trans people. No one told me transitioning was even possible. I just knew I wanted to grow up and be a man.

I fully embraced my masculinity at university and dressed in men's clothing. I faced some transphobia, but most students accepted me as a man. It was smooth sailing until my final year when a transphobic lecturer gave me the lowest marks of my life. I was acing every other class, so it's not like I wasn't trying. This lecturer just had it out for me. What could I do?

I told my parents what was happening, and they suggested I visit their church. I didn't see how that would help my grades, but how could it hurt? I agreed to join them one Sunday.

Like most charismatic churches, the atmosphere felt welcoming at first. Worshippers sang joyous melodies and chanted all around me, clapping their hands and smiling.

Illustration by Neil Badenhorst

The mood shifted when the presiding pastor started calling people up to the altar to receive their prophecies. Most were optimistic. One man was told he would accumulate wealth, another that he would own a shopping mall. I clapped for them and smiled, not sure I'd want the same. Then I heard the pastor call on me.

I had never met him before. How did he know my name? Everyone was in awe. I walked up to the altar, ready to receive my blessings. Instead, I was given hate.

The pastor told me I needed to change my "lifestyle" or my world would fall apart. Not understanding the euphemism, I asked him to elaborate. He jotted one word down on a piece of parchment and handed it to me. "Lesbianism."

Perhaps he thought writing it down rather than shouting it out would protect me from his congregants' scrutiny, but it made no difference. People saw my masculine gender expression and could guess what the pastor had in mind. The room began to whisper.

"I am who I am. I'm not willing to change," I told the pastor directly.

He called me into his private office after the service where a group of seven pastors were waiting for me. They took turns reading from the Bible, quoting verses they claimed "prove" that homosexuality is an abomination.

I'd always learned that the Bible emphasises love. My religious education teacher in high school specifically told us that Christians show light to the world through love. This didn't feel like love.

The following weeks were tense. I knew one of my parents must have told the pastor about my background. I felt betrayed. I was already battling with depression and suicidal thoughts. Trying to keep my grades up suddenly seemed like the least of my concerns.

Although my experience at the church was traumatising, it had a silver lining: it motivated me to become an activist.

Suddenly I understood the hardships so many queer people face at the hands of religious leaders. The shame, the embarrassment, the conversion therapies, the deliverance ceremonies, the exorcisms — I knew it didn't need to be like this. I started working to change pastors' mindsets, to convince them to provide us with the same love and care everyone deserves when they enter the house of the Lord.

I joined the Rock of Hope Eswatini in 2017 as a programmes officer with this religious outreach mission in mind. The Rock of Hope works to support and celebrate Eswatini's LGBTI community. We use religious advocacy and community engagement to create safe spaces for queer people and work to sensitise lawyers and police officers to ensure that our rights are protected.

Four years later I'm still sharing my story and engaging faith leaders to protect other queer people from the religious trauma I experienced. Many pastors I meet admit to discriminatory practices and vow to do better. The pastor who shamed me that day even reformed his ways and offered me a personal apology.

I've patched things up with my parents too. They support my work and stick up for me when other relatives make homophobic or transphobic comments. They even ask about my dating life!

Society fears what it doesn't understand. We can succumb to the haters' shame or we can stand tall and help others see our humanity. I choose to stand my ground and take pride in my difference.

DK Dlamini is the communications and advocacy officer at the Rock of Hope in Manzini, Eswatini.

BEAUTIFUL PIECES OF ART

GIGIE
Zambia

The year was 2013. I had just survived three years at a boys' secondary school in Lusaka and graduated. Now my family wanted to take me to church.

My uncle had convinced them I was possessed by a demon. How else could they explain my feminine gender expression? I'd been raised as a boy, but that's not who I was. I was a trans woman. I am a trans woman. They just wouldn't accept it.

On this particular Sunday morning, my mum's Pentecostal church was packed. The pastor called me up to the altar and started praying over me.

"Spirit of the darkness, come out, leave him alone," the pastor bellowed. My parents' faces glowed with the hope that I'd be delivered from the female spirit that "possessed" me. But I wasn't possessed. The spirit inside was my natural spirit. They just wouldn't accept it. They wouldn't accept me.

"All is well now," the pastor suddenly announced, his work apparently done, the demon supposedly gone. But I didn't feel any supernatural shift. I didn't feel any different. I just felt ashamed and embarrassed. My family and this pastor made me feel inhuman in front of a church sanctuary full of family, friends, neighbours, and strangers — just for being myself.

Illustration by Annabela Bekker

A month passed after my "deliverance ceremony" and I was still the same me. My gender expression hadn't changed. My gender identity hadn't changed. I was still the trans woman I was always meant to be.

I started reflecting on the humiliation my family and church had subjected me to. As part of my healing process, I started writing poems and speeches about human rights, about how everyone on this planet is a beautiful piece of art. I didn't want anyone else to be deemed inhuman because of their sex, sexual orientation, gender identity, or expression. I read my writing out loud, alone in my room, preaching to an imaginary audience. I didn't know a real audience was waiting to hear me.

Two years later in 2015, a friend introduced me to the Trans Bantu Association of Zambia (TBZ), an organisation that works to address the needs of transgender and intersex people across the country. TBZ invited me to a human rights focus group where we discussed some of the legal and social challenges trans and gender diverse people face. We also brainstormed ways to improve our safety and quality of life.

This was my first time interacting with so many trans people. I realised we all shared similar stories, struggles, and hopes for a better future.

Being around other trans people who understood me so well was inspiring. It sent me on a journey to create more safe spaces and positive social environments that welcome and nurture sexual and gender diversity.

Today I work as a programmes and advocacy officer for the Umotto Centre Of Culture, an artistic youth-led organisation that uses media advocacy tools to accelerate the human rights and visibility of sexual and gender minorities in Zambia. In short, we use art to spark change.

Since our founding in 2017, Umotto has engaged with more than 40 queer poets, artists, musicians, writers, and photographers to challenge patriarchal norms, values, beliefs, and structures that restrict our human rights. We also produce videos and documentaries that highlight the harassment and violence LGBTIQ+ Zambians face. As part of this process, we train young people to document their own fight for human rights.

Umotto Centre of Culture is now a true community of queer activists. Our fight is gruelling, but we know it's the only way to give ourselves and future generations of gender and sexual minorities a fair shot at equality and happiness. A luta continua.

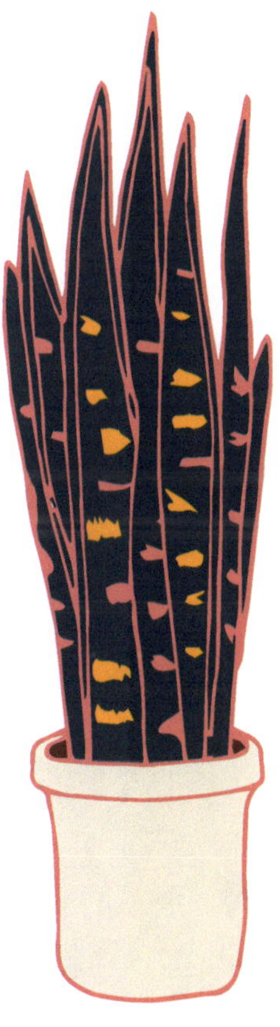

Gigie is a trans activist who works as the Umotto Centre Of Culture's programmes and advocacy officer in Lusaka, Zambia.

SEX WORK IS WORK
SAFE
JUSTICE
HEALTH CARE IS LIFE
RIGHTS
ASWA
TRANS

SEX WORK IS WORK, HEALTH CARE IS LIFE

CHARLES MUKOMA
Kenya

Kenya's Constitution declares health care a fundamental human right. As a trained health care provider, I know this is a lie.

Doctors and nurses in my country and across Sub-Saharan Africa routinely deny treatment to the vulnerable and marginalised people who need it most — sexual and gender minorities. In some countries, certain forms of health care are even illegal, such as providing hormone replacement therapy to transgender people. Witnessing these injustices in a profession I love is what first drove me to fight for LGBTQI equality.

In 2014 I started working with ISHTAR-MSM, a community-based organisation in Nairobi that advances the sexual health rights of men who have sex with men (MSM) by improving their access to medical care, including STI/HIV and AIDS-related treatment.

In my six years as a peer educator, field officer, and health care provider for ISHTAR-MSM, I heard heartbreaking testimony from sexual and gender minorities who sought medical treatment at local clinics only to receive bigotry and stigma. They were forced to either lie about their identities and try their luck at a different facility or to avoid treatment altogether. Many felt too traumatised to try again.

The consequences of this intolerance are staggering. Estimates suggest that half of MSM are HIV-positive in some regions. I learned the global

Illustration by Amina Gimba

scale of this tragedy at the Human Rights Campaign's Global Innovative Advocacy Summit in 2019 where I had the opportunity to discuss issues close to my heart with delegates from around the world. That's also where I started exploring the intersection between LGBTQI equality and sex workers' health rights.

I left ISHTAR-MSM in early 2020 to join the African Sex Workers Alliance (ASWA)'s membership and communications team. My hope was to use what I'd learned working with LGBTQI people to help sex workers, a similarly marginalised community that includes many sexual and gender minorities.

ASWA is a Pan-African coalition of sex worker-led groups that collaborate to amplify the voices of regional sex workers and to advocate for their health and human rights. ASWA envisions a world where sex work is recognised and protected under local and international labour laws. As ASWA and our partners say, sex work is work and must be decriminalised.

In poor countries and communities, sex work is the only feasible income source for some people, especially women and LGBTQI people. Laws that criminalise sex work make it harder for sex workers to negotiate terms with their clients or even carry condoms for fear that they could be confiscated as evidence of illegal "prostitution" during a raid or arrest.

Criminalisation drives sex work underground, making sex workers more vulnerable to exploitation and abuse. That's why ASWA and our partners are working so hard to decriminalise sex work across Africa and around the world.

Religious and political opponents routinely attack ASWA supporters for championing LGBTQI equality and sex workers' rights, but this backlash never stops our fight. We know what's right.

Health care providers have a moral and professional duty to treat LGBTQI patients. Lawmakers have a legal and ethical duty to protect sex workers by decriminalising their trade. End of story.

A growing number of international and regional NGOs are recognising the overlap in our fights for LGBTQI equality and sex workers' rights and raising their voices to help protect the legal, economic, and health care needs of our communities. These powerful new allies give us hope that change will come.

I'm an activist because I believe everyone deserves the right to work and the chance to lead a healthy life. My life's work is turning these beliefs into facts.

Charles Mukoma is a membership and communications officer at the African Sex Workers Alliance (ASWA) in Kenya

Make your voice heard.
Paint your palm to show them
that the time for legal equality is now.

#Reform53

Mercy Thokozane Minah

#REFORM53 — TOGETHER FOR LEGAL EQUALITY

NANDINI TANYA LALLMON
Mauritius

I'll always remember our first campaign event for #Reform53.

It was January 2020 at the New Zealand High Commission in London. One of my colleagues from the Commonwealth Youth Gender and Equality Network hit "play" on our campaign video, and our call to action flooded the room.

"#Reform53 — Together for Legal Equality" is an international advocacy campaign that works to end discrimination against women and LGBT people in 54 Commonwealth nations (the Maldives joined after our launch). I serve as #Reform53's legal adviser from my home in Mauritius.

Our video urged lawmakers to decriminalise same-sex relationships, end workplace discrimination, and increase political participation for LGBT people.

As the credits flashed across the screen and the lights came back on, I was overcome with emotion. My colleagues — other youth leaders from across the Commonwealth — moved in for a group hug, their faces beaming with pride. Our campaign had finally come to life.

We spent the rest of our launch week in London meeting with lawmakers, diplomats, faith leaders, and community leaders from across the Commonwealth, lobbying them to push their governments to reform discriminatory laws.

Illustration by Mercy Thokozane Minah

In February we presented the campaign in the Seychelles and Uganda. In March we spoke at an International Women's Day celebration in Papua New Guinea. We were seeing the world, spreading our message.

Then COVID-19 hit.

International travel came to an abrupt halt just as we were gaining momentum. I felt disheartened but never defeated. I'd been here before.

As a small island nation, travel to and from Mauritius is time-consuming and expensive. Growing up here, I relied on the Internet rather than airplanes to find and join other human rights activists around the world. I quickly learned that networking beyond my country is key to building successful humanitarian advocacy campaigns. This often involves working with international NGOs to create Mauritius-based chapters.

When #Reform53 started, I helped build a united front of coalition partners across Africa and beyond to boost our chances of success, but I also homed in on Mauritius, where same-sex sexual activity is still criminalised. I'm now working with LGBT Mauritians to use local courts to challenge discriminatory laws and policies and to promote the enforcement of equal rights laws and provisions that are guaranteed in our Constitution.

Winning each court case makes the next one easier and inspires more people to proudly and openly express their gender and sexuality. Through greater visibility, we aim to turn the tide from discrimination to equality in Mauritius and across the Commonwealth.

COVID-19 travel and safety restrictions required us to rethink our global #Reform53 campaign, but these hurdles never stopped us.

We quickly shifted our activities to the digital space, creating and sharing short films that underline the need for legal reforms that protect women and LGBT people. More than 60,000 people have watched our films on social media and another 15,000 have engaged with our webinar series. Social media has lit up with supporters sharing selfies that show our campaign logo drawn on their hands to emphasise our demand for legal reform.

I'm proud of the progress #Reform53 has achieved since pivoting online. When our target event, the Commonwealth Heads of Government Meeting, was postponed by one year to June 2021, we worried our campaign would lose steam. Instead, we've built momentum. We're now stronger than ever, eager and ready to showcase the public support we've won for legal reform that will bring about genuine equality for everyone.

Nandini Tanya Lallmon is the legal lead for the Commonwealth Youth Gender and Equality Network's #Reform53 advocacy campaign against discriminatory laws. She is based in Mauritius.

ABOUT TABOOM MEDIA

Taboom's media training, mentoring, publishing, monitoring, and response programs catalyse ethical journalism and public discourse around taboo topics. By shining light on taboos in the news, we aim to break their power. Our global work challenges stigmas, replacing stereotypes and discrimination with accuracy and respect. We facilitate responsible media coverage to safeguard and champion vulnerable communities and to advance human rights.

To learn more about our work and to download a free copy of this anthology, visit TaboomMedia.com.

ABOUT GALA QUEER ARCHIVE

GALA is a catalyst for the production, preservation and dissemination of information about the history, culture and contemporary experiences of LGBTIQ people in South Africa. As an archive founded on principles of social justice and human rights, GALA continues to work towards a greater awareness about the lives and experiences of LGBTIQ people in South Africa, and Africa more broadly. Thus their main focus is to preserve and nurture LGBTIQ narratives and culture, as well as promote social equality, inclusive education and youth development.

GALA publishes under their imprint, MaThoko's Books, a rare publishing outlet for LGBTIQ writing and scholarly works on LGBTIQ-related themes in Africa.

Taboom Media and GALA Queer Archive would like to thank
the following organisations for their support.

National Endowment for Democracy

Supporting freedom around the world

THE
SIGRID
RAUSING
TRUST